CHAMBERS PIVOT INDUSTRIES
PRESENTS

AMALGAMATE

A MIX OF IDEAS FOR YOUR BUSINESS

SUMMER 2016

GREGORY SCOTT CHAMBERS
EL PRESIDENTE

Copyright © 2016 Gregory S. Chambers

All rights reserved.

DEDICATION

To Wilson the border collie mix, who thinks I'm awesome

CONTENTS

   Introduction   i

1 Decision Making   1

- The Timeline
- Helping Clients Succeed
- Time to Sit and Think
- Being Out of Balance with FIT

2 Managing Your People   11

- Our People Are Our #1 Asset
- Improving Sales Meetings
- Acting Like a Movie Production
- FIT and Battery Levels
- Applying Strengths to Activity

3 Persuasion   23

- Help Your Customers Kick Butt
- Relationships and Breakthrough Products
- Minds Are Never Shifted on Data

Services   30

GREGORY S. CHAMBERS

This spring I spent 3 days in L.A. attending the Second Annual Million Dollar Consulting Conference hosted by Alan Weiss, PhD. The speaker list was impressive and world-class - uber consultant Alan Weiss, executive coach Marshall Goldsmith, speaking coach Victoria Labalme, branding expert Bruce Turkel, sales expert Lisa McLeod, positioning coach Mark Levy, marketing expert Robbie Baxter - but even more impressive were the high dollar consultants in the audience.

The theme I took from the conference is that our organizations are unique and when we celebrate that, and take those stories to the marketplace, the market rewards us. When we don't act in concert with our individual strengths or try to hide our weaknesses, we're punished.

That's the theme we're going to explore in these pages. Getting our business to be the best version of itself.

DECISION MAKING

The Timeline

We've been in this room for nearly 50 minutes now and I'm losing track of what we're discussing.

Carol is the first to speak up, "What exactly are we talking about?"

The room falls into stunned silence as heads go from looking at Carol to looking at the papers in front of them.

What exactly are you talking about?

It's a great question. I get myself invited to enough meetings to know that this tool will help you get through meetings faster and with more direction than you ever thought possible. It's a meeting performance enhancer.

The tool?

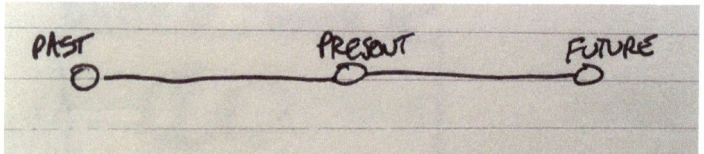

It's a simple timeline that you should revisit every time the meeting discussion drifts and you hear solutions, alternatives, directions and action items tossed around.

The timeline is split into three parts, the Past, The Present, and the Future.

The subtitles are the shortcut.

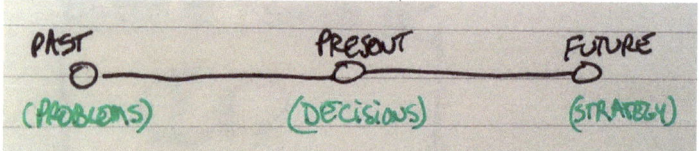

The Past is subtitled, Problems.

The Present is subtitled, Decisions.

The Future is subtitled, Strategy.

Let's roll through a scenario. The meeting is called to discuss hiring for a new position. It starts out with a stack of resume's that everyone should have previewed before the meeting and it's time to pick finalists for the position.

The first person asks whether the online submission software is working correctly because one of the internal candidates sent in a complaint. The second person asks about the hiring criteria, because two of the hiring committee members were talking before the meeting and it was suggested anyone from outside the industry not be considered. The third person asks the best format to use when discussing the finalists.

Sound about right?

The comments are all over the timeline.

Meeting's purpose? Decisions. Picking the finalists.

Software functioning? Problem. It's an event that happened in the past.

Hiring Criteria? Strategy. Disagreement on what we're looking for.

Comment format? Decisions. What's the best way to communicate in order to make a decision today.

How does this tool speed up your meetings? Because it helps you communicate on each issue using the right framework.

Problems are a result of something that happened in the past. Go back and find out what went wrong.

Decisions need to be made today. Use a framework for consensus building, and pick a direction.

Strategy is the future. Since it's unknown, focus on the defining knowns and preparing for unknowns. Preventative actions and contingent actions.

Framing meetings with this tool knocks meeting times in half. Try it.

Helping Clients Succeed

In sales and client development we are, at the purest level, working on one thing: helping our clients make a good decision. I used to say, "making the right decision," but over time I've realized that there are multiple paths to success so a good decision is what's best for everyone. Good decisions start with knowing where we are today, where we want to be tomorrow, and understanding the path to get there will be messy.

When surveying clients about what information we need from prospects to help them make a good decision, I get answers like "who will decide" and "budget" which are all good items that will help frame the decision, but if we're going to really get good at helping clients make good decisions, start with three key definitions.

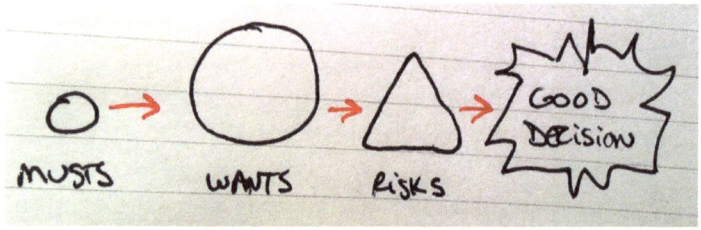

The first are the "must-haves." The client's non-negotiables. They are important because any right or good decision is going to have them included or the client isn't getting what they want. These must-haves come from the client and it's our job to be aware of them regardless of whether or not they are on our list of must-haves. For example, if a client is looking for an operations manager, they can express that must-have as "candidate must be able to get to the plant every day and in case of emergency." Even if I feel a nationwide search would be best, I am going to better serve my client by exhausting a local search first.

The second are the "nice-to-haves." These items aren't critical to the success of the decision, but will sound a lot like the must-haves. How do you differentiate? Try taking it away. "If we found someone who was perfect, but lived in another state and promised to be at the plant Monday through Friday, would that work?" If you can take it away and the client feels like they can still reach their goal, it's a nice-to-have versus a must-have.

Those are obvious to most of you and you do it naturally. The only trap to watch for is assumptions. To help your clients make good decisions, you need to hear them say it. No guessing.

The third definition is addressing risk. If you know their must-haves and have a list of nice-to-haves, the next step is to address risk. What future events or circumstances could derail this decision?

Going back to our fictional plant manager, let's step ahead and assume we find a local candidate that fits the must-haves and has a few of the nice-to-haves. What could derail their success? What if they perform below expectations? What if they don't integrate with the management? What if they get recruited away?

The risk questions seem endless, but they serve a dual purpose. They reaffirm the must-haves vs nice-to-haves, and they help make a good decision better because the client can think about contingencies and preventative actions and put the right plans in place.

Know the clients must-haves, their nice-to-haves, and help them address risk adds up to a good decision.

How Much Time Do You Have to Sit and Think?

Did you ever wonder where the concept of 10,000 steps comes from? This spring I was in St. Louis with my parents and they were both obsessed with their Fitbit devices. By the end of the second day, even I started asking, "how many steps?" That got me thinking about where this number came from.

It turns out that the surgeon general is behind the number because in the fight against obesity, being a couch-potato is more dangerous than being obese. Let me say that in a different way, your risk of cardiovascular disease if you are obese and active is only slightly higher than being normal and fit.

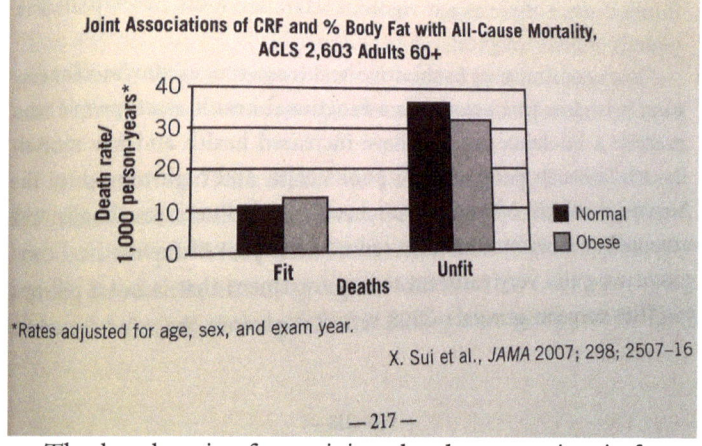

The break point for activity, the danger point, is fewer than 5,000 steps a day. Below that level, over time, your risk for an untimely death almost doubles. So, 10,000 is a big safe activity number.

Besides trying to imagine who among my friends is in the top quartile of obesity and top quartile of activity, this concept brought me back to thinking about time. Specifically, the time you spend in focused thought.

Here's what I want everyone to do: take 40 minutes, leave the phone at the desk, and go for a walk. Walk with nothing but your business and its problems on your mind. Take in all the sights and sounds, but don't distract your brain from doing its thing while you ambulate.

I have another inspiration for saying this. I just heard that Michael Lewis, author of books like Moneyball, is releasing a book on Daniel Kahneman and Amos Tversky. When I read Kahneman's book, Thinking Fast and Slow, I remembered him saying how valuable the long walks with Tversky were. Nassim Nicholas Taleb mentions his walks and their power in multiple articles and talks. In 2014, Frederic Gros even wrote a book about famous big-thinkers who walked, *"A Philosophy of Walking."*

The conclusion is to make time for yourself. An adult male around 6 feet tall walking 3 miles an hour gets in 2,000 steps every 20 minutes. A forty minute walk will not only help the cardiovascular system, if you spend that time thinking about your business, it will grow your business too.

Try it today. Keep these questions in mind as you walk and think about your business: Is what's concerning me related to an event in the past? Is it a decision I need to make today? A plan I need to make for the future?

Here's the secret, just let the thoughts bake in your brain. No need to dash off a memo or assign a team to fix things, just walk and think and feel and look.

Over three months, I predict you'll feel more in control of your business.

How do I know?

I walked about it.

Being Out of Balance with FIT

There are three main concepts behind FIT.

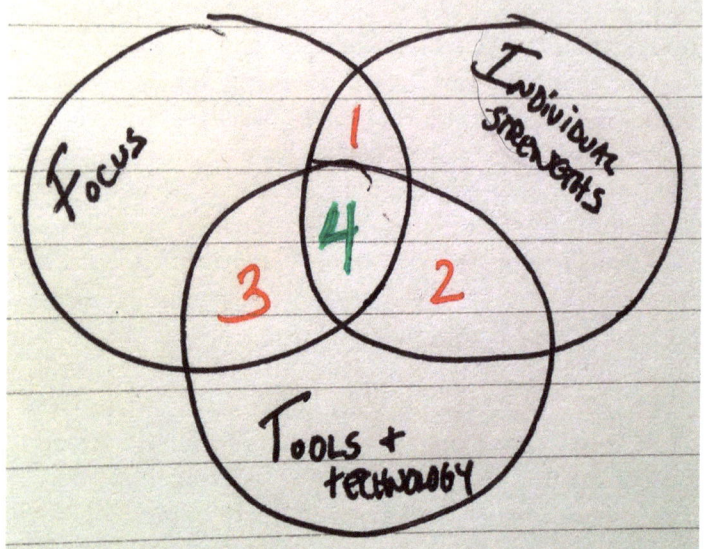

Focus is the ability to accurately and powerfully communicate your particular strategy to all levels of your organization. Not only communicating the task at hand, but especially the reasons why these activities are important. Describing the future in an emotional way leads to business growth.

The I stands for your team's **Individual** strengths. These are strengths that your team self-identifies through tools like the VIA Character Strengths test. Your management team's ability to harness those strengths and apply them to tasks, leads to business growth.

The T stands for using **Tools** and Technology to consistently get those tasks done. Technology is often the difference between doing nothing and something getting done. Consistency leads to business growth.

Let's look at what happens when your business is out of balance with FIT.

In position 1, you have Focus and you're using Tools built to help your people get more done in less time. There's a good chance that slow to no growth is ahead because your people are bought in. They are non-compliant because many of the business practices you're asking them to do just don't feel right. They're wearing a suit that pinches and pulls and it prevents growth.

In position 2, you have Focus and you're teaching your people to manage by strengths. There's a good chance you're experiencing growth, but it's coming in fits and starts. What was new and exciting becomes old and tired in a short time, and if new business activity isn't consistent, momentum never gets built. Sustained growth is impossible.

In position 3, you are managing by Individual strengths and using Tools and technology to increase activity. There's a good chance that slow growth is a result of your people wandering off aimlessly. They need Focus in order to justify pressing for the next level and stretching to achieve. Every port looks good to the ship without a destination.

When you have all three areas of FIT working in harmony, you're growth gains momentum and your people are working with flow.

To assess where your business is, take 10 points and assign them to where you think your team is today. Don't compare yourself to your peers and competitors, just look at your business and divide the points as you see fit.

Next, take 10 more points and decide how you'd like them to be split up in the future.

If you're out of balance in any area, start fixing it today. Contact me for resources.

GREGORY S. CHAMBERS

MANAGING PEOPLE

Our People Are Our #1 Asset

How do you treat your number one asset? What do you do to make sure they're cared for?

"We pay them well, we encourage time off, we provide extensive benefits, and we tell them every day."

Excellent.

I'm going to point out that you are the exception and not the rule. Most companies begin with the same statement, our people are our number one asset, and end there. A few back it up with action, the first of which is paying an above average wage. A few others go as far as encouraging time off and providing other such benefits.

None of them do what I'm about to suggest.

If you rely on humans to provide the value your organization offers to the economy, monitor these eight personal resources that every human being pulls from.

Financial - what goods and services can be purchased with the compensation you provide?

Emotional - are you offering training and tools to help control their emotional responses to their environment?

Mental - Are they in a position that challenges but doesn't overwhelm their brainpower?

Spiritual - Do they express a belief in a divine purpose?

Physical - Are there opportunities for health and mobility?

Support Systems - What does your people's back up support look like? Friends and family especially.

Role models - Do they have access to people that have been there before? Are those people nurturing?

Knowing the rules - Each group has unspoken rules. Is an effort made to expose them to the hidden rules of your company? Your customers?

Of those 8 personal resource areas, one is the easiest to manage, financial. It's inherently measurable and can be compared to industry averages. But where do you measure emotion? How do you measure mental? Spiritual?

Here's the thing: you don't need to measure them like you do financial. Not at first.

Step 1: acknowledge that you're interested in all of their resources.

Step 2: find a way to measure something, like by using a survey.

Step 3: Publish the results.

Step 4: measure again, on a regular basis.

Step 5: take steps to improve a single area.

Does that process look familiar? It's process improvement in action. And that's all I'm suggesting you do with your people, put in a process that helps them improve. If they really are your number one asset, investing in them will show up on the bottom line.

Just don't fall into the trap of thinking that it begins and ends with financial.

Improving Sales Meetings

The best way to improve sales meetings is to not have them.

Meetings are a cheat. You have them to disseminate a lot of information in one sitting, especially in sales. Housekeeping and paperwork are the norm, case studies, client scenarios, and discussion about helping clients make good decisions are the exception. So skip them.

If your sales management can't imagine life without meetings, then insist they use this communication tactic to disseminate information quickly and efficiently.

The tactic? Frame the meeting.

This will dramatically cut meeting time and people will understand and retain more of the contents. It starts with this phrase, "Today we are going to accomplish this: 1, 2, 3. . ." with all the key points listed in front of everyone. Either on the white board, or on a handout.

Here's why it works. It forces managers to have targets before the meeting. Plus, humans love lists. Completing the items on a list ties into our desire to show progress at work, and we love progress.

Once you've listed what's going to happen in the meeting, it's time for the first magic question.

"Before we get started, is there anything we need to discuss. . ?"

This question flushes out the best parts of getting together. Those side comments, burning questions, rumors, and success stories that derail most meetings. By framing what needs to happen in the meeting up front, then asking the first magic question, you're doing two things. Flushing out important issues that need to be discussed, and with the pressure of the actual agenda out in the open, the conversations are either brief or tabled for later. The transition is a simple, "enough on those topics, let's get through this," pointing to the agenda.

It works. But there's a second magic question you need to know about. It happens right after you complete the list.

"We're done, is there anything else before we go?"

It does two things for you, it's a natural question to signal a wrapping up of the meeting, and it provides continuation for the next meeting topics.

Using this framework and these magic questions, your meetings are done in less than 20 minutes.

The best part?

Your sales team spends too much time on relationship building and not enough time on the client's business. Running meetings with this framework teaches your people an effective way to communicate with their clients. "We become that which we see every day," says the wise man. Your people's meetings with clients will be more productive. Repeated bi-weekly, you'll see your people naturally using it in their presentations.

That's how to get the most from sales meetings.

Future Work: Acting Like a Movie Production

Getting the most from the least effort is my goal. I'm not advocating a lazy man's way to riches. The effort required is tied directly to the results desired. For some, the effort to get the most results is going to be much higher than others.

What I'm really talking about is speed. The most from the least effort, in the shortest amount of time. For the businesses I work with, speed has a direct correlation to the bottom line.

To get your results faster, act like a movie producer.

Think about how a movie comes together. You have talent, sometimes you add marquee talent, other times you have up and coming stars, and on the production side, in-house talent. What you don't have is permanence.

I read a story about the effectiveness of movie teams being tied to the number of people that have worked together on projects before compared to the percentage of new workers. If the production had a large percentage of people who had never worked with one another, the movie made less money than familiar teams. The conclusion of the article was that movie producers were best served with a certain level of familiarity.

You can take the same approach.

First, in your strategy sessions, break the objective off into a separate project. This will help with a few things:
- Goal setting
- Measurement
- Internal talent
- External talent
- The conclusion

How would this work in real life?

Let's look at a house remodeling project. The addition of a bathroom.

It could be handled in the daily course of home repairs. You've watched the remodeling shows, there isn't much to the project, but since you could only work on it some weeknights and weekends, it may take months to complete. Let's turn it into a project.

The goal is the finished bathroom. The measurements include speed, budget, and disruption. Your spouse is going to provide design direction, you're going to provide material transportation, and the kids keep the dog out.

The external talent is where you act like a movie producer. Instead of acting as a general contractor, use a general contractor but insist on mixing a few new subcontractors in. That gives you the best results.

The reason it works is the general contractor will have talent he is familiar with and they also know him. Some assumed knowledge is good and makes work move quickly, but too much leads to missed items. By adding in outside talent, you're forcing the team to increase their communication. That leads to a better result without the time kill of having people starting from zero.

That's what we're after. Getting the most from the least effort, in the shortest amount of time.

Fit and Battery Levels

The main concept behind fit is designing sales and marketing practices your people can live with. The main force behind applying those practices is your people's battery levels. Take a look at this graphic.

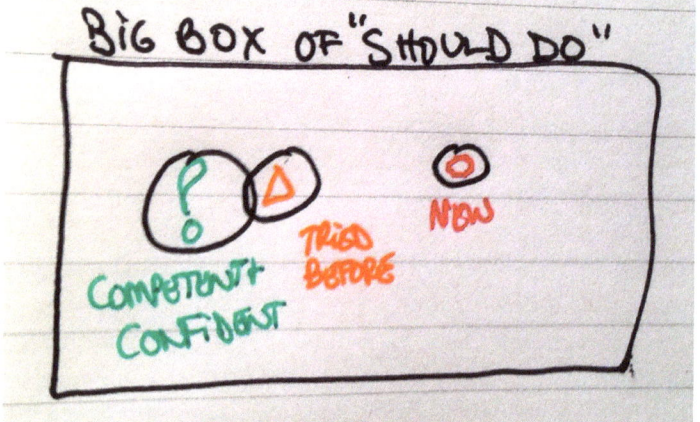

It's bounded by the box which I label, the "big box of what your should do." That box holds smaller circles of activities that your people feel competent and confident in, activities your people have tried before but are not competent or confident in, and activities that they've never tried before.

In reading Daniel Kahneman's book, "Thinking Fast and Slow," he splits our cognitive processes into two systems, System 1 and System 2, where System 1 is reflexive thinking, and System 2 is deliberate thinking. One of the interesting points he makes is that System 2 thinking, the deliberate thought processes, takes real effort and is physically draining.

Going back to the chart, label those activities your people are competent and confident in, System 1 activities. They are easier for your people, and don't drain their batteries much. On the opposite end are activities they've never tried before. Those require a large amount of System 2 thinking and will drain your people's batteries to dangerously low levels.

What does all this have to do with sales and marketing practices your people can live with?

Start with the assumption that any new sales or marketing activity is going to be terribly energy draining, so much so that if you require them to do it all day, every day, you'll lose them. It's too much.

However, since they are talented and on your team, they'll be willing to try some new things. It may only be simple activities, but it doesn't matter. What matters is that you have them apply their self-identified strengths to those tasks to make them more palatable. This is important because here's something else about energy draining activities: if your people aren't allowed to apply their strengths, they are less likely to even try them.

Each activity that they've done before and are allowed to use their strengths on, is battery enhancing. Keep them in those selling activities 75% of the time.

20% of the time you'll need them to stretch into newer activities that they've attempted before, but never had success with. It will be energy draining but manageable.

The last 5% of their time needs to be on activities they've never tried before. Assuming 1 hour a week of sales and marketing activity, you're looking at 3 minutes a week. Just enough to move an unknown to a known. They'll fail. They'll hate it. But they'll have tried it under your supervision with your feedback. Over weeks it will go from being a new activity, to being an imperfect activity, to being something they can live with.

That's how you manage sales and marketing practices that fit. You optimize your people's battery levels by monitoring the activities you ask them to do.

Applying Strengths to Activity

I have an exercise for you that brings the concept of FIT to life. Take a few minutes to complete it. There are two parts.

Part one: Think back to your early career. Imagine yourself at a time when you were young, headstrong, bright, but not experienced. Now, in that time period, you experienced an event that you were rewarded for. Take 8 minutes and write a quick story about it.

As you tell your story, answer these questions:
- What were you asked to do?
- How did you get it done?
- What was unique about how you got it done?
- Why did that earn a reward?

Use this prompt "One time, I was rewarded for an accomplishment when. . ." Go for it.

Times up. You've written some ideas down and the exercise should have been easy because we are looking for a single accomplishment, any type of reward, and no one else but you will read this. Plus, if you answered the four questions, you're excellent at following instructions.

Part Two: Now, I need you to head over to a website. Dr. Martin Seligman at the University of Pennsylvania has a project called Authentic Happiness. As part of his work with Christopher Peterson they developed the VIA Survey of Character Strengths.

It's a series of questions that you answer "Very Much Like Me" or "Very Much Unlike Me" - the questionnaire is 120 questions and takes 15 minutes to complete if you really stop and think about all the questions. I suggest reading the question and going with your instinct. There are no right or wrong answers. Your results are private.

https://www.viacharacter.org/survey/account/register

Go take the test now. I'll wait here.

Got them? Good. Now we're ready to finish the exercise, which will illustrate the importance of being true to yourself when it comes to growing your business.

Take your top three strengths from the Character Strengths test. These should ring true to you because you answered the questions. They are self-identified strengths. The questionnaire doesn't rank you against a population, doesn't pass judgment on how you see yourself, it simply ranks 24 character strengths based on your answers to those 120 questions.

To complete this exercise, take your top strength and go back to your story. Where can you find examples of that strength in your story? It's not surprising if your top strength isn't mentioned directly, so you might need to add some notes.

Do the same with strengths two and three.

Do you see places where your strengths helped you achieve your accomplishment?

That's why FIT works. We get better results when we use our strengths. Use this exercise with your team. It works

PERSUASION

Help Your Customers Kick Butt

Want to surprise and delight your customers? Help them kick butt at what they do.

I have a little illustration for you. I just bought a new camera. An entry level DSLR from Nikon. Let me show you the ad.

That's what I bought. I am endless possibilities. I want to kick butt. Look at that picture! I can see my boys and their friends in action. I can smell the chlorine. I can see my email inbox filling up with print requests from relatives.

This is what I got.

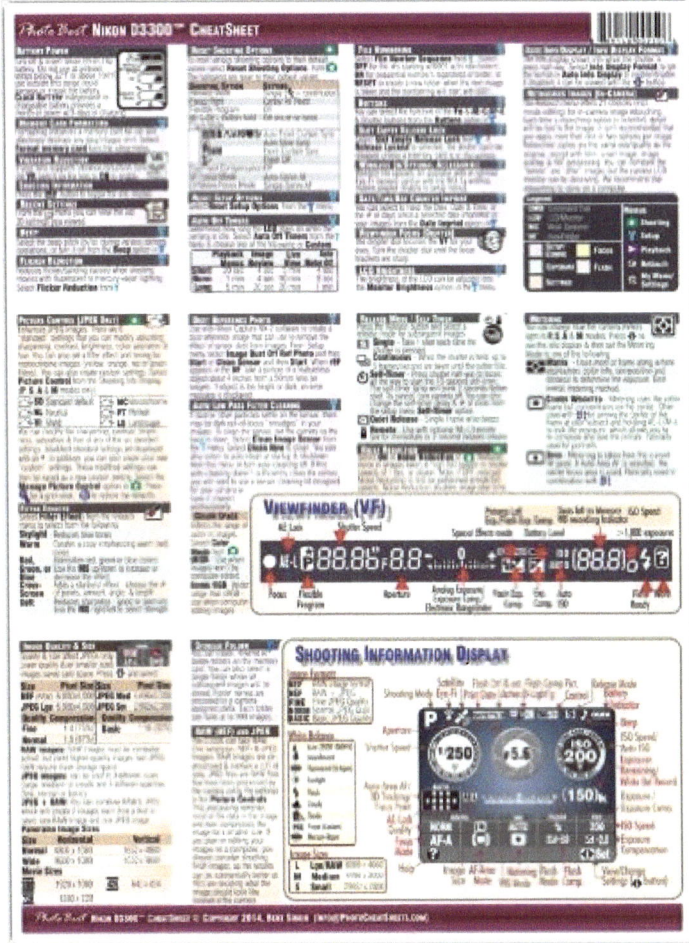

I have the tool to kick butt. I think. Not sure yet.

Don't do this to your customers. Make it easy to fulfill the promises you're people are making.

Help them kick butt.

Relationships and Breakthrough Products

What makes a breakthrough product or service? One that sets a high bar that you're known for and your competitors will have to reach for? Let me start by illustrating what I mean by breakthrough products with this grid from Alan Weiss, PhD.

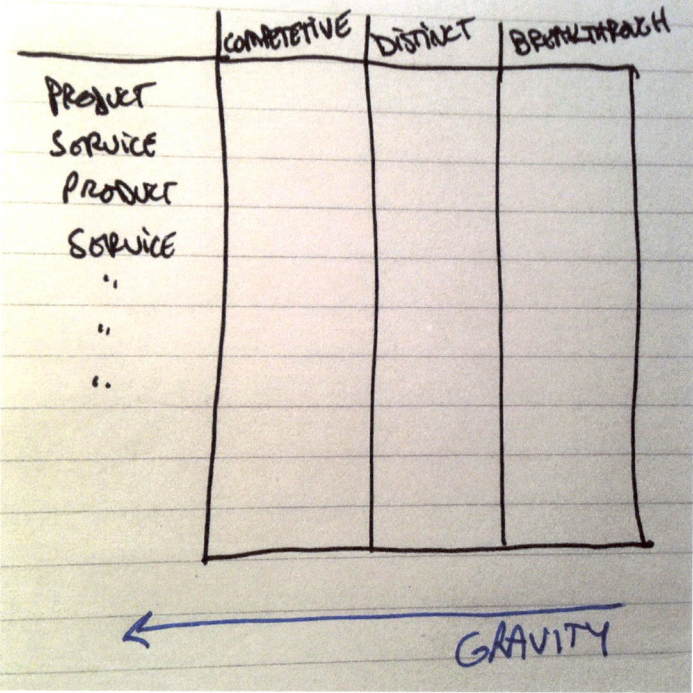

On the left of the grid, you list all of your products or services or offerings. Anything that clients invest in.

The way the columns work is this: on the left is a column labeled Competitive, which is all of your products, right? It's not a unique offering in the market, but it's a competitive one. It's competitively priced, competitively serviced, and if you laid it out next to your competition, it's well, competitive.

The second column is labeled Distinct, which are

products and services that are ahead of the pack. They have unique attributes that few competitors have. In workshops, clients have often defined the products in this section their "competitive advantage." They are what keeps you from being an also-ran in the marketplace.

The last column is labeled Breakthrough. These are distinct products and services that your clients can only find in one place. With you. It's expressed as, "Get me Greg," because no one else has it.

Take that list of your products and services on the far left column and put an X where that product is, according to your clients. Not how you perceive them internally, but how your clients perceive them. If it helps, use a little scale of 1 to 3 in each column with 3 meaning "more like this" and 1 meaning "less like this" in the category.

The Gravity arrow on the bottom represents competitive pressure. It pulls all of your Distinct products into Competitive and your Competitive products to a place that isn't even listed. Commodity.

Here's what I've noticed over time. All of the products that are listed in the Breakthrough column are 100% built on relationships. That either because you've slowly introduced the Breakthrough nature of the offering over time, or it's because the client was referred to you by someone familiar with your breakthrough service. Breakthrough products are rarely taken directly to the market. Especially in business-to-business environments.

Getting there requires investment. Investment in your people's ability to provide and communicate your breakthrough value. Investment in helping your customers promote your breakthrough products to others. Investing in earning peer-to-peer referrals.

Breakthrough products are the way to exponential growth and enviable margins. Plan to get there.

Minds Are Never Shifted on Data

We like to think of ourselves as evidenced based, scientific sorts, but we are, at our core, human beings. We reference data when we make decisions, but on close examination, we really use data to support our decisions.

Decisions are made on emotion. Good decisions are 2 parts emotion to 1 part logic, but most decisions can rely on emotion to get made.

Here's a boring example to prove my point.

Assume I have a University of Michigan educated lawyer that is practicing personal injury law because his father did, and his grandfather did before that. He's been working in the family firm for 10 years when he decides to leave and strike out on his own. In year 3 of his practice he has some big cases in the works. He's finally getting traction, clients are calling him, he can be pickier about who he represents, and he's getting cases that have large fees. Potential large fees because he's taking these cases on contingency. These cases can net him mid-six figure fees but they make take 4 or 5 years to settle.

He knows the drill. He's seen it before and it's all going according to plan, but a lot of his future success is hinging on those big cases closing. He's invested heavily in making this happen. He's tapped his savings, his wife's savings, and his house equity and it's making the home life stressful. The bank isn't interested in talking to him about a working capital loan because he hasn't established a steady income yet.

Along comes a special lender that says, "Hey, we'll consider those big cases as assets and give you some cash flow relief. We'll discount the value to something we can live with and only charge you 2.5% a month."

Some of you did the quick math and think "30% a year?!?" Here's the thing, he needs the cash. It's risky, but if doesn't take the risk, he'll never get the reward. Plus, he just got a call from a plaintiff with another big pharma drug defect claim. It's going to be expensive and take a long time, even if he works it with another attorney.

What's he going to do?

He'll make an emotional decision. We all do. Then we follow it up with this exchange.

"Hey, why did you do that loan? It's so expensive."

"Well, I did a lot of research and this company is one of the few that will use my work-in-progress as collateral . . .and if I only have the loan out for 3-6 months it's no worse than a credit card and if the car case settles . . .and if. . and if. . ."

What's not said is, "I can't fail. I can't go back to my Dad. I can't stand that these insurance companies are just dragging this out. I can't move the kids out of private school or leave my big house or look my wife in the face and ask her to do more. . ."

It's an emotional decision supported by logic.

It's how we work as human beings. Ultimately, no matter how large the company is that you're selling to, a human will be making a decision.

And if you only use logic and data, you will lose.

GREGORY S. CHAMBERS

Chambers Pivot Industries Services

Small to mid-sized businesses hire me to help them create more revenue. I do that in a very particular way. I help them design sales and marketing practices they can live with. Practices that fit. That are a natural fit for who they are.

See, the problem most businesses that size have with growing revenue is this: They're using growth strategies that just don't consistently work for them, based on their size and goals and disposition.

Why don't their strategies work well? I've been doing

this for many years, and I see at least three reasons:

One reason is that they're hemmed in by doing the same things that everyone else in their industry is doing, whether or not it fits them, and they can't break free. They do it like they've always done it but it's not giving them separation.

A second reason is the opposite of that, they are trying a new and shiny approach that is popular in the press. Like Fast Company or Inc. magazine. The challenge there is many shiny, new tactics are great for selling books, but aren't vetted in the real world.

The last reason is that they try to emulate what the big successful companies have done, without understanding that giant organizations are fundamentally different. Compared to a growing SMB, those companies have unlimited time and resources. They can make any approach work.

All three of those problems are examples of what I consider a "bad fit" – like wearing the wrong size shoes, it's un-natural and it may work, but it's keeping them from reaching their potential. Instead, I encourage companies to consider who they really are: humans, real people with strengths and weaknesses. I help them design practices that are a natural fit for them. I help them figure out what works best.

If your company's sales and marketing effort would benefit from learning about FIT, get in touch with me at http://www.chamberspivot.com

REFERENCE MATERIAL

I encourage you to learn more from the authors and consultants referred to in this booklet.

Alan Weiss Ph.D can be found at
 http://www.alanweiss.com

Mark Levy has been indispensible in helping me clarify my thinking and sharpening my writing. Find him at http://www.levyinnovation.com

My website is http://www.chamberspivot.com and I keep a blog there that is updated each week. My new newsletter on FIT gives you 4 quick ideas each Friday to use next week. Sign up today.

ABOUT THE AUTHOR

Greg Chambers is the founder of the sales-and-marketing consultancy, Chambers Pivot Industries LLC.

He helps entrepreneurial companies create sales-and-marketing practices they can get excited about and are a perfect fit for their cultures.

Greg began his consultancy in 2012, and has worked with clients in nine industries, including ecommerce, finance, and healthcare. He coaches clients on how to build revenue through practices like online-and-offline lead generation, new market penetration, database marketing, and referral training.

Before opening his firm, Greg was a serial entrepreneur. He led the expansion of the cult apparel company, Mad Gringo, and co-founded the lead generation company, GoLeads.

Greg is also a novelist. His thriller, *"The Legend of Mad Gringo,"* follows a Hawaiian shirt-wearing protagonist who quits his corporate job and is forced to do battle with "The System" and "The Syndicate."

Greg lives in Omaha with his wife, three children, two cats, and a dog.

www.ingramcontent.com/pod-product-compliance
Lightning Source LLC
Chambersburg PA
CBHW040818200526
45159CB00024B/3026